Beauty and the BEAST

Book Design & Production: Slangman Kids *(a division of Slangman Inc. and Slangman Publishing)*

Illustrated by: "Migs!" Sandoval
Translator: Ofra Obejas
Copy Editors: Julie Bobrick
Nili Hirsch
Tami Kamin-Meyer

Copyright © 2006 by David Burke

Published by: Slangman Kids *(a division of Slangman Inc. and Slangman Publishing)* 12206 Hillslope Street, Studio City, CA 91604 •USA • Toll Free Telephone from USA: 1-877-SLANGMAN (1-877-752-6462) • From outside the USA: 1-818-SLANGMAN (1-818-752-6462) • Worldwide Fax 1-413-647-1589 • Email: info@slangman.com • Website: www.slangman.com

"Migs!" Sandoval
✳ our illustrator ✳

Miguel *"Migs!"* Sandoval has been drawing cartoons since the age of 6 and has worked on numerous national commercials and movies as a sculptor, model builder, and illustrator. He was born in Los Angeles and was raised in a bilingual household, speaking English and Spanish. He currently lives in San Francisco where he is working on his new comic book series!

D1228094

N10: 1891888-943
N13: 978189888-946
...nted in the U.S.A.

10 9 8 7 6 5 4 3 2 1

Order Form

Preview chapters & shop online!
www.slangman.com

SHIP TO: _____

_____

_____

_____

Contact/Phone/Email: _____

Method of Payment (Check one):

☐ Personal Check or Money Order
(Must be in U.S. funds and drawn on a U.S. bank.)

☐ VISA ☐ Master Card ☐ Discover ☐ American Express ☐ JCB

Credit Card Number

Signature

Expiration Date

QTY	ISBN-13	TITLE	PRICE	LEVEL	TOTAL COST
English to CHINESE (Mandarin)					
	9781891888-793	Cinderella	$14.95	1	
	9781891888-854	Goldilocks	$14.95	2	
	9781891888-915	Beauty and the Beast	$14.95	3	
English to FRENCH					
	9781891888-755	Cinderella	$14.95	1	
	9781891888-816	Goldilocks	$14.95	2	
	9781891888-878	Beauty and the Beast	$14.95	3	
English to GERMAN					
	9781891888-762	Cinderella	$14.95	1	
	9781891888-830	Goldilocks	$14.95	2	
	9781891888-885	Beauty and the Beast	$14.95	3	
English to HEBREW					
	9781891888-922	Cinderella	$14.95	1	
	9781891888-939	Goldilocks	$14.95	2	
	9781891888-946	Beauty and the Beast	$14.95	3	
English to ITALIAN					
	9781891888-779	Cinderella	$14.95	1	
	9781891888-823	Goldilocks	$14.95	2	
	9781891888-892	Beauty and the Beast	$14.95	3	
English to JAPANESE					
	9781891888-786	Cinderella	$14.95	1	
	9781891888-847	Goldilocks	$14.95	2	
	9781891888-908	Beauty and the Beast	$14.95	3	
English to SPANISH					
	9781891888-748	Cinderella	$14.95	1	
	9781891888-809	Goldilocks	$14.95	2	
	9781891888-861	Beauty and the Beast	$14.95	3	
Japanese to ENGLISH 絵本で えいご を学ぼう					
	9781891888-038	Cinderella	$14.95	1	
	9781891888-045	Goldilocks	$14.95	2	
	9781891888-052	Beauty and the Beast	$14.95	3	
Korean to ENGLISH 동화를 통하 ENGLISH 배우기					
	9781891888-				
	9781891888-				
	9781891888-				
Spanish to ENGLISH					
	9781891888-				
	9781891888-				
	9781891888-				

Sales Tax *(Cali...)*

Prices subject to change

SLANGMAN® KIDS
(a division of Slangman Publishing)

**** TO PLACE AN ORDER...**
Phone: 1-818-752-6462 • Fax: 1-413-647-1589
Email: info@slangman.com • Web: www.slangman.com
12206 Hillslope Street • Studio City, CA 91604

(FORM 071606)

Dedication

The entire "Foreign Language Through Fairy Tales" series is dedicated to all the children of the world.

It is through their understanding, appreciation, and celebration of our differences that the world will become a better and safer place for us all.

One thing to remember...

The words in **green italics** throughout this fairy tale are words you've already learned in previous levels! Do you still remember what they mean?

1

bat
בת

me'od
מאד

Once upon a time, there was an *abba* who had an eldest [daughter] named Julie, a middle **bat** named Tessa, and a youngest **bat** named Belle. He loved them [very much]. While getting

ready for a long [trip], he asked each **bat**, "What can I bring you from my **masah**?" "A [ring] to wear around my finger," said Julie. "I'd like a [necklace] to wear around my neck." said Tessa.

masah
מסע

taba'at
טבעת

sharsheret
שרשרת

3

Bevakashah ←
בבקשה

shoshanah ←
שושנה

But Belle, who was the most *yafah* of all said, "[Please]. I don't want a **taba'at** to wear around my finger or a **sharsheret** to wear around my neck. All I want is a [rose]." Her *abba* replied,

4

You shall each receive your [gift]." "Oh, *todah!*
Todah!" said each **bat**. Then their *abba* mounted
his [horse], and they shouted "Have a good
masah, *abba!* We will miss you **me'od**!"

matanah
מתנה

sus
סוס

As the *abba* rode off, each **bat** shouted again, "*Le'hitra'ot, abba! Le'hitra'ot!*" until he was out of sight. Days later, it was time for him to return. So he first stopped to buy a **taba'at** for his eldest

bat to wear around her finger, a **sharsheret** for his second **bat** to wear around her neck, but he waited to get closer to his **bayit** to look for a (garden) where he could find a **shoshanah** for

gan
גּן

Belle. After a few hours, he saw a magnificent **gan**. He got off his **sus**, walked into the **gan** and picked a **shoshanah** that was the most *yafah* he'd ever seen. At that very *rega*,

the *delet* to the *bayit* opened and a [beast]
came out and ran toward him. "Who stole
a **shoshanah** from my **gan**?" exploded the
chayah. "Oh, **bevakashah**, [sir]!" said the

chayah
חיה

adon
אדון

9

abba. "**Bevakashah**, **adon**. Don't hurt me. I promised my **bat** that I'd bring her a **shoshanah** as a **matanah** after my long **masah**. It was just ONE **shoshanah** from your **gan**!" "It's still

stealing!" said the **chayah**. "I will spare your life if you bring me the **bat** you speak of by noon in six days. Here she will live the rest of her life." Naturally, the

tzohorayim
צוהרים

abba was very upset by this request, but he promised to return with Belle at **tzohorayim** in six days. When he arrived home, each **bat** rushed out to greet him. He gave them each

the **matanah** they'd asked for. Each **bat** was
very *smechah* and shouted, "*Todah*, *abba*!
Todah!" "*Al lo davar!*" he replied. But he
was still upset because he had to tell Belle

13

**ani ohev
otach**
אֲנִי אוֹהֵב אוֹתָךְ

about the promise he'd made with the **chayah**. "Belle, I love you. **Ani me'od ohev otach** and want you to be *smechah*. But I must tell you what I have done..." Her *abba* went on to explain

what happened that day and about the promise

he had made. He warned her about how ⟨ugly⟩   → **mechu'ar**

the **chayah** was, but Belle felt very responsible   מכוער

because the **shoshanah** was a **matanah**

she'd requested. So, she agreed to go. The days passed quickly until it was time to leave. As Belle and her **abba** mounted the **sus** and rode off, she was very **atzuvah** to say **le'hitra'ot** to her sisters.

After a **masah** that took several hours, Belle and her *abba* arrived at exactly **tzohorayim** as instructed. They got off the **sus** and approached the *bayit* of the **chayah**.

17

Shalom
שלום

The **delet** opened slowly and they walked in. "Hello!" said the **abba**. "**Shalom**!" But there was no answer. Then they saw a **shulchan** filled with food in the middle of the **mitbach**.

It looked like someone was having a *mesibah*!
Just then they heard a deep voice say, "**Shalom**.
This [food] is especially for you. **Bevakashah**,
enjoy!" Not wanting to be impolite, they began

ochel
אוכל

19

eating the magnificent **ochel** before them.

And so many desserts! Belle was so excited and

already busily counting them. "...four, five,

six. And such wonderful desserts they were!

arba
ארבע

chamesh
חמש

shesh
שש

She counted them again just to make sure, "*Echad*, *shtayim*, *shalosh*, **arba**, **chamesh**, **shesh**! It was true! **Shesh** delicious desserts all for them! They had never seen such wonderful

ochel in their lives! Suddenly, they heard footsteps approaching. There he was – the **chayah** himself. Indeed, he was truly **mechu'ar**. Scared, Belle said, "**Shalom**,

adon and **todah** for the delicious **ochel**."

"**Al lo davar**," replied the **chayah**. He

seemed very ⟨kind⟩ toward Belle. Her

abba was permitted to come visit her

nechmad
נחמד

every week which made her very **smechah**. He gave Belle a kiss, mounted his **sus**, and said, "*Le'hitra'ot*, Belle. **Ani ohev otach** my **bat**!" and rode off back to his **bayit**. At that very **rega**,

the **chayah** turned toward Belle and said,
"**Bevakashah**. What's mine is yours. I will
return every day at **tzohorayim** to see you."
He then quickly ran off, leaving Belle alone.

Because he was so **nechmad** toward her, Belle was no longer afraid, and was even *smechah* when he came to visit at **tzohorayim**. Every day, they laughed more and more and enjoyed

sharing stories with each other in the **gan**. But one day, the **chayah** didn't arrive at **tzohorayim** as usual, so Belle went to look for him. She walked outside into the **gan** and there he was

lying on the ground lifeless. Belle cried, "Oh, why did you have to die, my **chayah**? Why did you have to die?!" She gave him a kiss on the cheek and suddenly right before her

eyes, he awoke and was transformed into a **_nasich_** who was very **_yafeh_** indeed! He explained to her that an evil magician had changed him into a **chayah**. Only the kiss

from someone who had great **ahavah** for him could change him back to the **nasich** he used to be. The next day at **tzohorayim**, Belle became his **ishah** and they all lived happily ever after.